IMPROVE YOUR COMMUNITY AND IMPROVE YOURSELF

JANEL CLARE STERBENTZ

Only a life lived for others

is a life worthwhile.

ALBERT EINSTEIN

1

INTRODUCTION

THINK about how fulfilled you felt the last time you did something kind for someone else. Maybe it was the joy of volunteering for a nonprofit, the pleasure of contributing to a worthy cause, or the gratification of helping a stranger. Being prosocial strengthens our sense of relatedness and fulfills some of our most basic psychological needs.

Supporting others is a central part of humanity; it brings us together and improves society as a whole. Studies have found numerous examples of how making a difference, in small or large ways, benefits us immeasurably. There are countless stories about people who accomplished everything they wanted yet still felt unsatisfied. It wasn't until they assisted others that they truly found the gratification that had previously eluded them.

The following is a story by Stephanie Downs, CEO of Uncaged Innovations and co-founder of Material Innovation

Initiative.[1] She tells how volunteering gave her a sense of purpose and transformed her life.

"It all started for me about 15 years ago. I had worked really hard through my twenties to build my career and reach a point where I thought true happiness existed. Then, one day while driving home, it dawned on me: I had everything I thought I had wanted to reach bliss, but I didn't feel any different. I wasn't happier; I actually felt pretty empty inside.

"After a lot of soul searching, I decided that I needed to 'give back.' I remember choosing this with such confidence, as if doing this one additional thing would complete the magical puzzle. I'm happy I went down the path, but I laugh when I think about it in hindsight.

"I searched the internet for ideas. I looked into volunteering at an orphanage (none to be found since we have a foster system). I volunteered for a bit at a homeless shelter, but it didn't feel like the right fit for me. Then I decided to respond to an ad from a local animal shelter to help walk dogs and clean kennels.

"I was greatly enjoying the mental break from the daily stress of my life (at the time, I was just one year into starting my first business), but within a few months, I was on the board of directors and running the main annual fundraiser. It was a ton of work, but I wouldn't have changed it for anything.

"My journey began at what was then the Table Mountain Animal Center (now called the Foothills Animal Shelter) in Golden, Colorado. Within a year, I became a vegetarian, after it dawned on me that I could not snuggle one animal while it shivered in fear and then eat the flesh of another. I decided to step away from my business, work for an animal rights organization, and eventually start my own charity.

"What I thought was going to be a tiny piece of my life ended up being the answer to the entire puzzle. I had found happiness in giving back, and it is a high I can't even describe. Whether you volunteer a few hours a week or decide to make the leap and dedicate your life to helping others, I promise it will change your life in a way no money or material objects can."

HOW DOES HELPING OTHERS HELP ME?

IF THE WORK genuinely improves people and the environment, it undoubtedly helps you. These benefits are both direct and indirect.

Researchers claim that performing altruistic acts is a primordial behavior passed down through our genes. Numerous studies have shown that those who engage in activities that aid others receive many mental and physical rewards, such as a longer lifespan, greater self-esteem, and better mental health. This remains true irrespective of socioeconomic class, gender, or age.

One peer-reviewed research paper looked at 73 different studies assessing how volunteering benefits the individual. Most studies show that volunteering leads to an improved mood, increased self-reported fitness, more mobility, and longer lifespan.[1] Volunteers devoting just one to two hours each week gain these benefits.

Lengthens life and boosts the immune response[2]

Low levels of social connection have been linked to an increased risk of death from cardiovascular disease, infectious diseases, and cancer. These effects are proven even when controlling for physical health. Loneliness and social alienation raise the likelihood of dying sooner: by 26 percent for loneliness, 29 percent for social isolation, and 32 percent for living alone.[3]

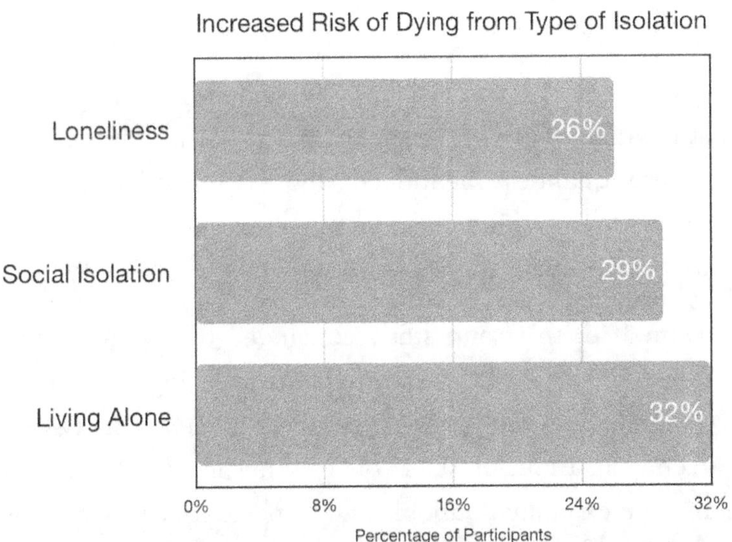

One study by Cigna concluded that loneliness among Americans rose to 61 percent in 2019, up from 47 percent the year before.[4] Mental and physical health issues, living alone or far away from home, a lack of social care, and infrequent meaningful social activities all raise the risk of loneliness.

Becoming involved in activities that are important to you allows you to connect with those who have similar interests. One study by UnitedHealthcare found that volunteering improved 75 percent of participants' emotional well-being.[5] Thirty-four percent of volunteers said it relieved debilitating diseases. Volunteers are 78 percent more likely than people who have not volunteered in the previous 12 months to believe they have control over their health.

Improves self-esteem, decreases depression, and reduces problematic behaviors[6]

Assisting others magnifies an individual's sense of purpose. It strengthens skills and social connections, which boost all of these qualities mentioned above. Supporting others allows us to stop thinking about ourselves and our problems. This reduces anxiety and stress.

A UnitedHealth Group study concluded that volunteering resulted in 79 percent of participants lowering their stress levels and 88 percent having greater self-esteem. Ninety-four percent felt a greater sense of meaning in life, 89 percent gained an expanded outlook, and 85 percent developed new friendships.[7]

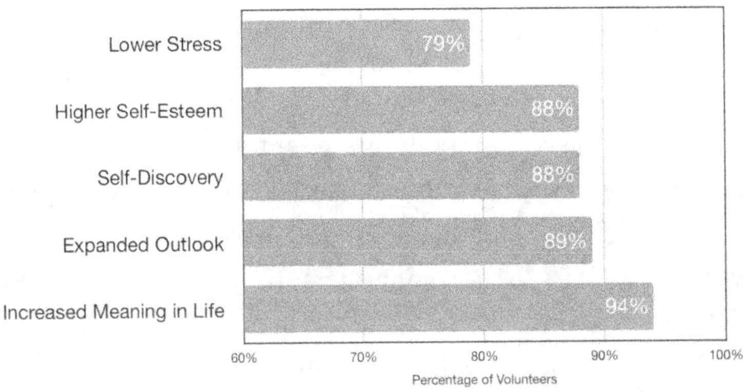

Research shows that performing kind actions helps people who are socially insecure feel more confident.[8] It alleviates fears of potential rejection, temporary stress, and discomfort. In one study, non-volunteers in social situations did not gain these positive effects experienced by those who helped out.

To gain the full benefits, it's best to witness the impact of your work on others. This is especially true when you directly receive praise from those who express their gratitude. This is why volunteering in person can be more gratifying than remote work or projects physically removed from those affected.

Boosts the feel-good hormone oxytocin[9]

Participants in a longitudinal study completed a variety of charitable tasks over two years. They also recorded stressful events and physician-diagnosed physical ailments. Those who performed the prosocial activities generated higher levels of oxytocin. Oxytocin is a hormone created naturally in the brain. The hypothalamus, a small area at the base of the brain, produces it, and the pituitary gland nearby secretes it.

Oxytocin assists the body in adapting to a variety of emotional and social circumstances. It generates antidepressant-like effects in animals. Studies have also shown that when levels of this hormone increase in the body, we are able to better manage stressful events.[10] So those who are engaged in more altruistic activities acquire the positive mental boost of increased oxytocin levels.

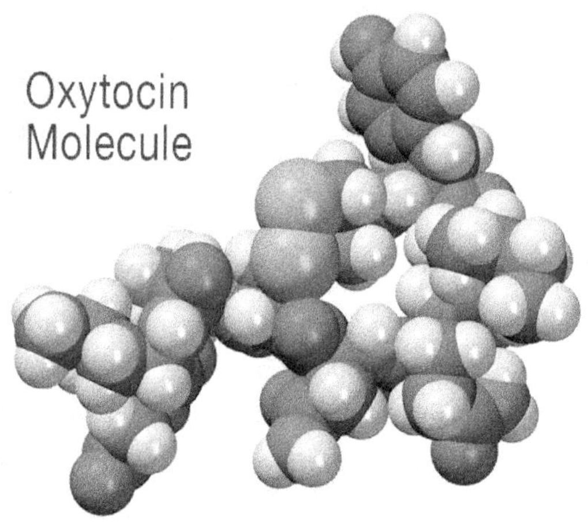

Reduces the risk of cognitive impairment[11]

A 14-year study concluded that for those over 60, regularly volunteering over time reduced the odds of experiencing neurological deficits by 27 percent. Strong social interactions can help protect memory and cognitive function as you age.

Mental stimulation and moving around are also essential factors.

Decreases chronic pain[12]

This research concluded that people with chronic pain who volunteered had less pain and a stronger sense of purpose. It was the meaning that they assigned to their act of service that affected the amount of pain they felt. The effects were not only long-term but also immediate. Various studies have found that the act of giving deactivates parts of the brain that react to painful stimulation.[13]

When we volunteer, we choose what we want to work on, as opposed to paid work that doesn't necessarily have a meaningful connection to our interests. This activity, which builds a support system based on shared interests, is beneficial both mentally and physically.

Lowers blood pressure and reduces inflammation[14]

A Carnegie Mellon University study discovered that adults over 50 who volunteered 200 hours or more each year cut their incidence of high blood pressure by 40 percent. The type of volunteer activity wasn't a factor so much as the amount of time spent volunteering. In the United States, more than half of all people have hypertension. Heart disease is the leading cause of death in the US. Only about one in every four people with hypertension has their blood pressure under control.

Chronic stress can keep the body in a high-stress condition for longer than it should. Although stress may or may not affect blood pressure, how you deal with it does. People who overeat, smoke, or drink too much alcohol to manage stress develop elevated blood pressure over time. Healthier coping strategies such as exercise, talking with others, and generally being active can help to relieve the effects of high blood pressure.[15] As people age, they may have fewer opportunities to interact socially, and volunteering opens up the pool of potential new friends. So perhaps this is why it has such a positive effect on blood pressure.

You get the extra perks

Organizations often thank volunteers by offering them complimentary goodies, including free tickets to events they organize. You meet new people whom you otherwise wouldn't have encountered and gain new skills for free. You also get the inside scoop about what's going on in that area. You get to try new things and participate in new activities.

Susan J Noonan, MD - Physician and author of *Managing Your Depression: What You Can Do to Feel Better* and *When Someone You Know Has Depression: Words to Say and Things to Do*[16]

Dr. Noonan graduated with an AB from Mount Holyoke College, where she received the Abbey Howe Turner Award for excellence in biology. She has a doctorate in medicine from the Tufts University School of Medicine and a master's degree in public health from the Harvard University School of Public Health.

Dr. Noonan has volunteered at the Maxwell V Blum Cancer Resource Room of the Massachusetts General Hospital, Boston, MA, for the past eight years. She assists patients with obtaining information and provides counseling. In 2006 she was given the MGH Volunteer Service Award recognizing her exceptional service.

"The first thing to know is that when you volunteer, you commit to making yourself available to a person or an organization for a period of time, say two or four hours per week, on a regular ongoing basis. You do it in small steps, not all at once. You become accountable to others for showing up on time and ready to function at some moderate level. They will depend on you for that. It's a big step.

"This was good for my depression, and I'll bet yours as well. The person or organization does not know you, doesn't know that you don't feel well, and are feeling depressed. It's actually possible to fake it, to 'act as if' you're feeling well for short periods and establish new relationships with new people.

"Second is that when you volunteer your time regularly, it gives you a sense of purpose and accomplishment that perhaps you may have forgotten. You feel better about yourself, and your self-confidence improves. You come to feel needed and appreciated for what you do for others. That is important to have, and I found that it's a different feeling from when you have a paid job. You can also learn new skills that you can use in other areas of your life.

"Volunteering gives you the opportunity to think of something and someone else rather than being swallowed up by your own overwhelmingly depressing negative thoughts. Seeing the problems that other people have, made my problems seem less intense in comparison, at least for a short while. Having lived through depression also gave me greater patience and empathy in my volunteer interactions with others.

"When you volunteer your time, you have to pull yourself together, get off the couch and out of the house. You have to present yourself to others in a pleasant manner. That's all a huge effort when depressed! First, you have to get showered, wash and style your hair, and get dressed in clean, pressed clothes. It's usually 'business casual,' not sweats, tees, or jeans. The reason for this dress attire is out of respect for the people you are helping, the organization you represent, and yourself. This is all good for your depression.

"The volunteer function you perform depends on your interests and skills. It might be reading to children in the town library, delivering food to elderly shut-ins who can't get out, assisting the blind with errands, helping others with their computer skills, working with dogs in a dog shelter, or guiding people through your local museum. There are a ton of possibilities. It all involves interacting with people you don't know. This helps you develop your social skills and offsets the tendency toward isolation in depression. It can produce anxiety at first, especially if depression has caused you to be more isolated, but over time that will get better.

"You might think, 'I'm too tired, too disorganized, too depressed, and don't have anything to offer people.' You may not know what to do or where to start. Just remember – action precedes motivation. Get started, and the interest and motivation will follow. I urge you to take small steps, two to four hours a week, in an organization where you have or previously had some interest or currently have some skills to offer.

"Here's how I did it: I began volunteering at the cancer resource room of a large academic hospital, two hours a week at first, then four hours a week. It wasn't a downer, as you might think. At first, I was nervous because with my depression I had trouble reading, remembering, and concentrating. I thought that would interfere with my ability to function in the volunteer role. I had to make workarounds, write things down to remind myself of certain tasks, and practice being relaxed in my interactions with others.

"I persisted and was determined to succeed, but on a few occasions I had to excuse myself when I was admitted to the hospital for depression. I never told them the real reason for my absence, but eventually we all became friends, and they figured it out. They were remarkably accepting and understanding of my illness. It turns out they all had someone in their lives with depression, and they didn't mind as I had feared! It all worked out okay because two years later, I received a rare volunteer service award."

HOW DO I START?

THE FOLLOWING activity will help you see how you can spend some of your free time in a gratifying way while helping to solve the problems around you.

The first step is to identify your interests and what you feel can be improved.

It may help to first quiet your mind. So if you like, sit it in a peaceful place and meditate for a few minutes.

1. Sit comfortably on the floor or in a chair.
2. Observe your breath.
3. Your mind will inevitably wander. Don't judge – bring your attention back to your breath.
4. Relax your muscles and observe how your body feels.
5. Set an alarm for a few minutes and begin.

If you are reading this as an ebook, you can either print these pages or draw them yourself.

Now think about issues or **problems** you experience in your life, observe in your community or in the world. Write down five of those and why they are important to you. Be specific. Indicate whether it's a personal, local, national, or global issue. Write those in the boxes below.

Think about the activities and **hobbies** that you like to do. Or **skills** you enjoy practicing.

What are your **interests** and topics that you like?

Input values from 1 to 10 in the small boxes next to each of the 11 items listed, 1 being least important to 10 being the most important to you. You can use each number more than once.

Are there any similarities or connections you can make between these items? Draw lines from the problems to those hobbies and interests that connect or have potential connections. When examining these potential connections, think about ways you can utilize your interests and hobbies to solve the problems.

HOBBIES   INTERESTS

Scoring

In the chart below, along the top row, list the problems that you wrote above. Then add the hobbies and interests that you connected to those problems in the following rows. Include the scores of each and add them up.

The scores on the bottom row show which issues are most important to you and interest you the most. Add each of the entries across and place those numbers in the first column. These scores show how vital the subjects are in relation to the problems.

Analysis

Problems					
Hobbies					
Interests					
Total Score					

List the top three **problems** with the total scores, highest score first.

. . .

1.

2.

3.

These problems are probably always in the back of your mind, so once you start working on them, it will relieve some of your stress. Now write down the hobby and interest that got the highest scores from the left column.

Hobby/Skill:

Interest:

Fill out the following:

What can I do to help out with (input **problem** number 1 from above):

by using my **skill** of:

.   .   .

and incorporating my **interest** in:

If you can devise an activity or work with an existing organization that fulfills all of these characteristics, you'll have found highly gratifying and beneficial work. If you can't come up with a matching activity, or it doesn't feel right, you can input any of the other top-scoring items in any order.

Repeat the above sentence; fill it in as many times as you want to come up with other activities. There are resources at the end of the book that can help you find organizations to support you. Now answer the questions below.

What goals do I want to meet through my activity?

How will my activity work toward my goals above?

Action

Once you have an activity you're satisfied with, let's answer some questions:

How much time do I want to devote?

. . .

What role do I want to have?

Do I want to start something on my own or work with an existing organization?

Do some research to see if anyone else is already working on it. Write down some organizations here you can work with or that can give you some support for your project.

Write down some of the steps you can take to start your project.

Note: If those issues with the highest scores are personal, it's advisable to address them for your mental or physical well-being. Based on the importance of the personal issue, you may want to address it before moving on to those problems outside of the private realm.

This doesn't mean you have to necessarily solve that problem before moving on. Rather, it's an indication that you probably need to put some energy into that concern, whether writing down your thoughts, speaking to a friend or therapist, or taking steps to solve the issue. It can even be your top project if that feels right to you.

· · ·

"There's a hospital near my house where you can volunteer over the summer. I'm interested in healthcare, so I'm exploring to see whether this is what I want to do when I grow up. I've been interested in this field since the middle of this past school year. I enjoyed learning about biology, and I like science, so I thought it'd be cool to volunteer at a hospital.

"The orientation was fun; they gave us a tour of the hospital. The first three times that you volunteer, they stick you with someone to show you around. It was so much fun! We could take tellys, which is a heart monitor, to wherever they needed to go. We could take dietary meals to the patients who wanted food. We could ask patients whether they wanted water or coffee, if they were allowed to have that. We were able to take medical records to wherever they needed to go. We were able to escort people who needed wheel-chairs. I could take specimens to the lab.

"A lot of the time, I was the only teen volunteer in the ER. I got to see four traumas. I got to shadow in the corner, and if I felt woozy or something, they said that it's a good idea to sit down. First, it was hard for me to watch that type of stuff, but then I got used to it, and it was not a big deal to me. I would recommend it if you are interested in going into the medical field.

"Even if you're not interested in the medical field, it's a great way to make new friends and have new experiences. It's so cool, the things that you can experience at a hospital. Growing up, I enjoyed watching 'Grey's Anatomy,' so seeing that in person and seeing those people work was cool to me. I understood some of the terms because I used to watch the show. I made so many new friends; I learned so much stuff. I had so many new experiences that I will never forget, and I definitely want to continue volunteering."

4

VOLUNTEERING

ACCORDING to Wharton professor Cassie Mogilner's findings published in the *Harvard Business Review,* people who donate their time actually feel like they have more of it.[1] They perceive they have achieved something valuable and believe they will do more in the future. They sense time to be more wide-ranging due to their increased competence. In the end, they feel more self-assured and productive.

About 75 percent of workers who volunteer through their work say it gives them a better impression about their workplace. Through volunteering, 87 percent of employees notice enhanced technical and time management competence. Ninety-two percent of respondents agree these practices improve their people skills and teamwork, and reinforce relationships.[2]

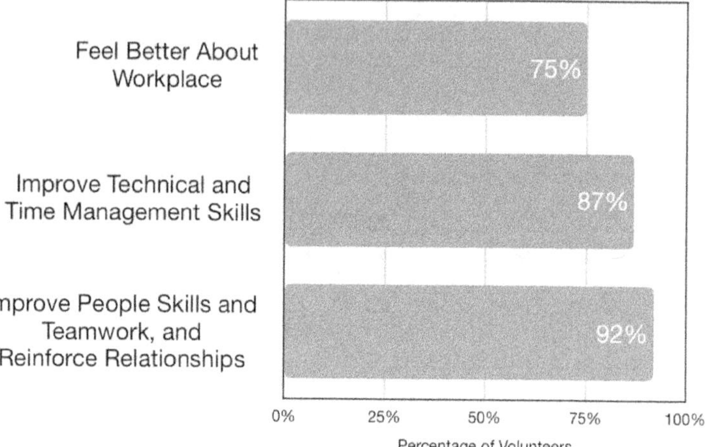

Volunteering allows us to have new experiences and participate in larger, more meaningful environments. According to the 2018 Volunteering in America survey:[3]

- 77 million US adults (30 percent) participated in volunteer work through an association.
- Americans volunteered 7 billion hours or 167 billion dollars worth.
- Many more lent a hand to friends and relatives (43 percent) and performed good deeds for their neighbors (51 percent).

Volunteers serve in their neighborhoods at higher rates than non-volunteers. They are more likely to speak to neighbors, repair problems in the community, join civic groups, attend public meetings, address social issues, and vote — while those who have never volunteered watch 436 more hours of television a year.

Americans have also contributed a sizable sum to humanitarian groups. Volunteers gave to good causes at a rate of 80 percent, compared to just 40 percent of non-volunteers. In the United States, half of the population donated to a charity organization in 2018.

Donating to philanthropic organizations has been shown in many studies to have long-term positive effects on one's well-being.[4] Your brain chemistry alters when you donate money to a cause you value. Scientists can observe in real time how contributing increases activation in the brain's reward systems through brain imaging analyses.

When an individual donates, two regions of the brain become more engaged. The first is the mesolimbic pathway, which is where the feel-good dopamine chemicals are released. The second area stimulated by giving is the brain's subgenual region, which is involved in forming social bonds.

How Does Volunteering Help the Community?

Volunteers play an integral part in the day-to-day operations of most nonprofits. These organizations would not survive if it weren't for volunteers. Most municipal institutions, associations' boards, and various commissions also rely on volunteers.

A large number of nonprofit organizations work to solve problems that must be addressed but are not being dealt with for various reasons. Many issues should be resolved by governments; however, the governments don't have funding, are inefficiently run, or are corrupt, and the money is taken instead of used for the community.

Volunteers are crucial to fill those gaps and build essential connections between citizens, governments, and companies. When people help out in their communities, they develop a sense of pride and they feel they've invested a part of themselves in their communities. This creates safer, stronger, and more cohesive neighborhoods. The enhanced connections between people increase the flow of ideas. The volunteer gains valuable skills while improving their physical and mental well-being. This in turn benefits society as a whole.

Salman Hossain - Tech product and innovation expert in Thailand[5]

"Volunteering is not just a mere extracurricular activity or even a way to do something good for someone; it's much bigger. It's larger than life, where you devote yourself to a cause that is bigger than all of us. To me, that probably is the best definition of volunteering. I make sure that my true worth, when it comes to volunteering, is always doing it for society, doing it for the greater good of people and the community to which I belong. That is the only reason I do what I do when it comes to volunteering, and this is going to help you see how I've taken the different steps in my life to engage myself through volunteering.

"Let me walk you through a summary of my volunteering experiences. Once I had a new definition and a bigger purpose to the whole idea of volunteering when I came back from the United States, I started going back to the community. I began working in the slums on education for young children in primary school. I saw that these children were hardly getting a quality education. They were far from having the ability to dream big for themselves while living within the limits of the slum life.

"Then, because I was so passionate about education and helping these children, instead of working the typical corporate job, I ended up taking a job at a very early stage non-governmental organization (NGO) that was starting to work with the country's youth. They were helping them build the nation of the future. I joined them as the founding management team member. I ended up training the next generation of Bangladeshis, some of the brightest young kids, making a big difference not just in Bangladesh but beyond. At that organization, I established the first community service project, which is now the standard. Every single student is involved in various community projects in that area.

"After finishing the community service and working for the NGO, I realized I didn't want to lose touch with those children, so I created a fundraising program with the same youth who were part of the program. I also raised funds for eleven children to get sponsored for the next two years to continue to help them stay in education. Because of my community service experience, I started to feel stronger about my country. I wanted to do something bigger than just community service in the field; I thought I had a higher calling.

"At that very point in time, I found out about TEDx, a global independently organized TED event. It was coming to Bangladesh for the first time, and at that very instant, I said, 'I want to volunteer.' This eventually led me to become one of the core organizers creating the largest and the biggest TEDx in 2012. Having worked at TEDx and given a significant number of my valuable hours in life, I ended up using it to promote Bangladesh.

"Then, Bangladesh did not have a positive image because of the lack of communication and the media presence. My goal was to find the hidden talents, create a positive story around Bangladesh that was always missing, and create a better narrative of our life in Bangladesh.

"Having worked on TEDx, I met great people, which led me to also volunteer for another project by Google. When Google started a community initiative called Google Business Group, they began launching these chapters in different countries. As they were entering Bangladesh, I became one of the Bangladesh chapter co-founders called Google Business Group Dhaka. I ended up working to help increase the adoption of technology in bringing the community together. It led to empowering startups and pretty much pioneering the scene in Bangladesh that we see today. It's growing and accelerating at an unprecedented speed.

"Eight to ten years ago, having worked with Google Business Group also led me to meet some fantastic people through all this volunteering and giving these countless hours. By helping people find what they were looking for, I also landed a job by meeting a friend that headed the organization. It was the most prominent advertising technology company back home in 2012. That led me to continue to stay relevant in my work in the community. It was astounding to be recognized by the World Economic Forum with an award for the first Global Shaper in the country.

"Had I not worked all those years in the community – in education with the slum kids, with that NGO to help train the next generation of the community, at TEDx to help promote Bangladesh, with Google to help increase the adoption of technology and bringing the community together, they would not have recommended that I become the first Global Shaper in the country.

"This kept getting better and better as every time I needed to promote anything about Bangladesh, I got more help coming from all directions. This work with TEDx also eventually led me to get a Gates scholarship to the TED event – an all-expenses-paid trip to San Francisco to be part of significant tech events. I learned firsthand how they organize it, so when I returned to my country I could once again give back to my community.

"That brings me to the very end, where I want to highlight some of the key benefits of volunteering and what exactly it teaches us, in addition to simply having a great time being part of a bigger picture. Volunteering teaches us kindness and humility. I think there's no other work that can teach you empathy the way volunteering your valuable hours does. Instead of giving it to your family or yourself, volunteering your time to others teaches you authenticity. When you're going out there and trying to help people, those on the receiving end will recognize if you're not being authentic. There is no transaction here, just pure service. So volunteering teaches us the true meaning of authenticity that I haven't found anywhere else in my life.

"Volunteering also helps you become more grateful when you see that you are in a much better position in life than many other people who are not as privileged as you. You learn to be more grateful about the things you have in your life, and I've become more thankful on so many occasions just simply by volunteering.

"Volunteering also teaches us leadership and ownership. Because of volunteering, I learned that leadership is an activity; it's not a position. I realized that anyone could go into the community and take the lead in driving change instead of waiting for someone else to give you authority, position, or power. Last but not least, volunteering gives you a global identity. You must find extra time in your life for service, your full-time job, and your family life.

"If you are a university student, I highly recommend you put aside some time for giving back to the community. If you are a corporate professional working on a startup, make sure you put aside some hours every week and every month for giving back. If you are a parent, please tell your kids to get involved instead of simply playing on their PS4s, Xboxes, computers, and smartphones. There's an excellent opportunity for them to learn how to do different types of skills. If they don't understand how to give back to the community, a whole part of humanity might be lost during their upbringing.

"If it weren't for that series of events that I was involved in after office hours, spending countless hours volunteering by giving back to the community, I wouldn't have learned many things that I know today. I wouldn't have become the person I am today. I wouldn't have had the opportunity to meet some of the amazing people who eventually became my friends, for which I'm incredibly grateful."

5

TIPS FOR VOLUNTEERING

THE FOLLOWING suggestions can help you to have a more successful and enjoyable experience volunteering.

Work with organizations that have transparent aims and results

Harvard psychologist Michael Norton, a co-author of the book *Happy Money,* discovered that we are more satisfied when we are more certain our time and money lead to improvements.[1] Keep in mind that sometimes your time and energy may not get the results you're expecting. That's okay; it's a chance to learn and move forward.

Volunteers are essential to nonprofits, but poor management can lead to volunteer frustration. This may be why more than a third of those who volunteer one year do not volunteer for any nonprofit the following year.[2] Nonprofit leaders must build a more systematic approach to ensure volunteers are valued and the organizations meet their needs.

Managers can establish a weekly one-on-one meeting with volunteers to discuss expectations and experiences.

Those organizations with the most success retaining volunteers make it easy for them to sign up and get the job done. They prepare for those assisting, and they are organized. They make a concerted effort to be welcoming and show their appreciation for those who are helping. They also provide activities that allow people to get to know one another. Volunteers appreciate the guidance and comprehensive training to ensure they do the job well.

Find an organization that matches with you

You are more likely to be successful in and continue contributing to a group that you mesh with. Different organizations may have the same goals, but perhaps they go about things differently. Learn the specifics of each organization and ask yourself what is important to you.

For instance, say you want to help a group working for animal welfare. Perhaps the focus of one organization is to make sure stray animals are not roaming the streets, while another concentrates on raising money to support plant-based meat companies. Both have the end goal of helping animals, yet they approach it differently.

On the other hand, many organizations will likely be open to your ideas related to their needs. It doesn't hurt to reach out, ask to meet up, and discuss your thoughts. They are often grateful for help in all forms, and thus willing to support you.

Consider the location of the organization. Is it convenient enough to keep you volunteering there on a regular basis? The closer the place, the more likely you will regularly see the fruits of your labor. This type of positive reinforcement keeps a person going back. Volunteering with a friend makes it easier for some to remain motivated. In addition, many organizations offer remote work if you would rather not go in person.

Assess your role

It's a good idea to begin with a meeting to discuss your skills and interests. Talk about what you hope to gain and what you would like to accomplish during your term. If you feel like you are giving more than you are getting, speak with your manager to see how they can better tailor your work to satisfy both of your needs.

Often organizations are tempted to give new workers jobs that nobody else wants. This may be especially true when a volunteer will be there for a short period. Every organization has some tedious work it needs to do, but if you find yourself consistently doing tasks you don't want to do, it's time to speak up about it. If even after discussing with management and your expectations still aren't being met, don't be afraid to inform them you don't feel like it's the best fit.

Frank Bruno - Ideological supporter, advocate, and volunteer for the blind and vision-impaired community[3]

"I was coming back from visiting my sister in the suburbs on a metro train, and I arrived at Union Station at about one in the morning. There was a couple there who were visually impaired or blind, I don't know for sure which one. They were pawing their way along the wall because the Amtrak guide who was supposed to meet them didn't show up. He had his hand on her hand, and she was behind him.

"She was lugging a suitcase, he was dragging a suitcase, and he was touching the wall trying to find a place to ask a person a question, like a stand or a ticket counter. At one in the morning, nothing was open. I looked at them again, and I thought, this is crazy, so I went up to the gentleman and said, 'Excuse me, sir, can I help you?' And he said, 'An Amtrak person was supposed to meet me here, and we're trying to get on a bus to go to Detroit. They were going to take us to the bus stop upstairs, and no one was there.' I said, 'Well, let me do this – I'll take you upstairs, and let's see if the bus comes.'

"We finally got upstairs, and I asked someone who was waiting by the bus stop, 'Is the Detroit bus coming?' And they said, 'Well, it might have already been here.' To make a long story short, the Detroit bus had not arrived yet. I went back and got them on the bus.

"These two people took the chance to venture out into a world where everything is an adventure. They didn't know where the next step led to because they couldn't see anything. I don't go to church a lot, but I decided to go to church the next day. Behind the bulletin where they do all the advertisements was an advertisement for an organization that helps blind people. I thought, this is highly coincidental.

"Being an analytical person by trade, I thought, well, this is abnormal in my life of dealing with numbers and quantities. The coincidence is too high, so I called the number, and I started volunteering. That was it. Additionally, my youngest brother had Down syndrome, and he passed away. Because I had lived with a disabled person in my younger years, I understand how a complex disability affects the entire family unit, the community, and society.

"Disability is something that is here. It will remain here, and we need to handle it in a very ethical and logical way. Who's to say what would have happened to that couple, but I can only imagine if I was in a city that I wasn't familiar with at one o'clock in the morning, and I was looking for the transfer bus that I might have missed, I would be distressed whether I could see or not. I can understand the importance of providing just that little bit of assistance and care.

"I think I, like most people, take what I have for granted. I took for granted the ability to get off that train from the suburbs, rode the escalator upstairs two floors, started walking home, crossed the street with stop lights, and felt reasonably safe in that endeavor.

"To appreciate who I am and what I have, a comparative study is necessary. I'm not as rich as many other people, and I know that many other people have more things to deal with than I do. We need to address those things because if I were in that situation, I would feel helpless.

"I think it's essential for us to acknowledge that feeling of helplessness and vulnerability. I think it's also important to humanize that and empathize with that feeling, which I think is why people become volunteers. You're uplifted, and you're encouraging another person. Both individuals benefit from it. You pick up a homeless kitten, and you bring it to the shelter. The creature benefits you. You feel good walking home if you teach a person how to deal with the bureau-cracy or help them deal with an issue over a delinquent bill or something they weren't expecting.

"Yes, it's going to make you feel good because you helped another person go through life's complexities. Life becomes negative by the number of complexities we have. If you have twelve complexities in your life, it's more damaging than an individual who only has two. The more complexities you can remove from a person, you're making the person feel freer, and freedom is a wonderful feeling.

"So yes, mentoring, helping – whether it's paying bills, reading to them, or going down to city hall and fighting because the property tax bill was inaccurate. Or calling the IRS and saying they did file their tax return and all the other things that I've done as a volunteer. It's produced a positive character in me. I don't believe I'm altruistic or egotistical, but I do believe that it makes me feel good. It feels great when you leave them knowing that they smile, or you've made them laugh three or four times during the two-hour visit. You can't help but feel good. When you make another person laugh or make their life easier, you have to feel good about yourself.

"I think the interesting thing about me is that for years I felt good because I had a good job and people paid me to give them advice. This time I didn't get money, and I still felt good. I've probably been volunteering for the visually impaired and blind for three and a half years now, and every group of people has their own cultures and subcultures.

"Some visually impaired people don't ask for help, and some people with vision do ask for help. I've had cases where people have said, 'No, don't grab my arm. I don't need your help now.' You could be offended by that, or you could say, well, that's okay, that's just a part of the learning curve. By the time you've worked with an individual, it's no different from developing a friendship. You could start a friendship, and you don't know a lot about that person, but there are things about that person that you know you like, but you don't know the total individual. As you get to work with the visually impaired person, they will let you know what they want and don't want.

"I had one person, as an example, who was extremely rude when I was trying to help, and I said I wouldn't do that again. There's no need to be rude, so you need to tell the person that you also have feelings. I want to help, but I have feelings, so let's work together. If you don't want me to correct your grammar, that's fine but tell me in a better way, and that friendship gets built based on these foundations of understanding. Because as we go along and develop relationships, there are ebbs and tides. We don't know the individual totally, but that's part of being creative in the friendship process – we end up gaining understanding.

"That's the key word – understand. *Understand* how that person wants to be your friend, and that's when the friendship takes off. I volunteered for two other nonprofits over the years that became very important. One was an organization that supports animal rights. I think there are humane ways of dealing with our relationship with animals. The piece that bothered me the most was the cruelty to them. When you're just cruel to a creature, that is something that tells me the person's spirit is tainted. Since the poor creature cannot defend itself, I felt the need to volunteer.

"In many ways, animal abuse leads to human abuse and society abuse and the ability to accept abuse in general. If you accept abuse in general, you start diminishing cultures and things that you don't know. It led to volunteering with a group in Washington DC that was attempting to lobby for something related to the laboratory use of animals.

"The last one was a group of teachers on the West Coast. When I lived on the West Coast, I would get together with this group of 3,500 teachers. Some of us had the job of locating children who could not buy a musical instrument or pay for music lessons. We wanted to bring out the creativity that a lot of children have. The music teachers were willing to then give discounts on music lessons or buy cheap violins.

"The group was willing to buy tickets to a symphony that the kids had never attended. It allowed them to expand their ability to appreciate and love a thing like music that they couldn't pursue because of economic limitations. Some parents avoided the offer because they knew it would hurt their children when they couldn't afford a violin. So they tried to dissuade children from actually pursuing music. It constricted them. It's sort of like the inability of a community to expand their well-being because of restrictions due to economics or geography.

"I primarily got involved with helping the blind to provide access to people who probably did not have access. When you look at a person, you don't look at just their eyes; you look at the entire individual and say, you know I could help in other areas. I could help them feel better because of this thing or the other, which has nothing to do with eyesight. I was involved in a case where a visually impaired person got into a cab, and as soon as the cab found out that he was using a tap card, they drove him eight blocks and kicked him out of the cab. We knew that shouldn't be allowed so we issued a complaint against the cab company.

"The young person was smart enough to take a picture of the license plate and the cab number, and we went down to city hall. We asked what they could do to help us, and we got nowhere. I'm not saying that to criticize; I don't know why we got nowhere, but they said they couldn't help. So we went to another government agency. Finally, they found out that he was visually impaired and was using a tap card. That is a system whereby the cabbie has to wait for his money for 30 days. They settled with the cab company for 500 bucks.

"When we talk about those kinds of things, it's going beyond the scope of the volunteer job. It produces a part of me that knows this system is not working. We've got to fix it. Unless you get people to confront their complacency, we're not going to change the rights of the disabled person. Complacency kills; it destroys even the organizations and governmental units that we developed to help it. Even though I'm just one person retired from his job who volunteers very little, I take that as an insult because the person who was kicked out of the cab is someone I consider a friend. Even though I'm only teaching him to do his homework, that was something very important that came up in his life. It's important that we get involved without fear."

6

TURN YOUR PASSION INTO MONEY

THOSE OF YOU who want to make money doing what you love, read on. There are many ways that volunteering can lead to paid work. New research from the Corporation for National and Community Service (CNCS), on the connection between volunteering and jobs, shows that unemployed workers who volunteer have a better chance of finding employment.[1]

- Volunteers have a 27 percent higher chance of obtaining jobs after being laid off than non-volunteers.
- Among people who do not have a high school diploma, those who volunteer have a 51 percent better chance of finding work.
- Among people who live in rural areas, volunteers are 55 percent more likely to find a job.

CNCS discovered that volunteering is linked to a universally better chance of finding work, regardless of gender, race, age, location, or job market conditions. According to Census Bureau statistics, the number of new businesses in the United States increased by approximately 24 percent in 2020 compared to 2019.[2] Also in 2020, 56 percent of Americans believed they would be more secure working for themselves than in a conventional workplace, up from 32 percent in 2011.[3] In this uncertain employment market, volunteer experience can give you an advantage over other job seekers.

The *Wall Street Journal* found that more than 80 percent of human resources executives believe that professional volunteer service distinguishes a prospective employee and increases their chances of being recruited.[4] However, fewer than half of college seniors view volunteerism as a way to improve their expertise for potential careers. While 26 percent of Americans aged 20 to 24 are unemployed, a 2015 Bureau of Labor Statistics analysis found that just about 18 percent volunteer, the lowest level of any age group.[5]

When you help an existing organization:

- Often they will provide free training so you gain valuable skills and knowledge that you can add to your résumé.
- It looks good on your résumé because it shows you are civic-minded and care about those around you.
- It's an accessible, low-pressure environment in which to get to know others and network. These connections may lead to paid work that piques your interest.
- It allows you to try out different types of jobs to explore what you prefer doing. You can find out if you are inclined to work for a smaller or larger organization, whether you enjoy collaborating in groups, and the type of work environment you favor.

- You can gain valuable references for future applications.

If you start your own organization:

- You'll attract others who want to achieve the same goals, and these connections can lead to paid jobs you enjoy.
- If you're doing valuable and in-demand projects, people might eventually want to pay you.
- Since you're passionate about this, putting in extra time will come naturally.
- If it's something that also helps your community, the benefits you gain will propel you forward.

Perform a job search to see if you have some of the required skills. Look at the job requirements and take steps to gain more expertise.

It's a good idea to keep your day job while you explore new endeavors. Do some research and start small. You'll slowly gain confidence and knowledge to build your clientele. Make sure to know your market and offer something in demand. Take your time and figure out whether there are enough people out there who will pay you for your product or service.

Soon enough, you'll learn whether this is something you really enjoy doing. If you're not used to working on your own, it may be challenging to stay on track and focused. It helps to set a schedule along with realistic goals. Sign up for mixers and professional get-togethers with people in the fields you're interested in. You can learn best practices from them.

The US Small Business Administration has offices around the country that offer guidance to help businesses get started. SCORE, a nationwide nonprofit, matches business advisors with entrepreneurs. See if you can find a co-working space near your home. Many not only provide a place to work, but also organize resources and events that can help you get on your way. Some companies prohibit employees from doing outside work, so be sure to check your contract.

Lance Eaton - Writer, educator, instructional designer, and social media consultant in Arlington, Massachusetts[6]

Lance has earned degrees in history, criminal justice, American studies, public administration, and instructional design. He's currently working on his Ph.D. in higher education at the University of Massachusetts, Boston.

"Volunteering has been a vital part of my life since I was young. In high school, I volunteered for a summer as a junior counselor at a YMCA camp. Granted, at age 14, it sounds more like free labor and a summer babysitter for my parents, but I was also giving back to the camp that I had gotten so much out of while growing up. In my senior year of high school, my favorite teacher (Mr. Metropolis) required us to volunteer 20+ hours in his AP US history course.

"In volunteering, he required us to keep a log of our experiences. Sure enough, while volunteering at one event (which brought me back to my elementary school), I chanced to fall into conversation with a woman from an under-funded local preschool. My conversation with her led me to volunteer at the school for the rest of the school year, doing more than the minimum required time and continuing to volunteer there for several years after.

"All of these volunteering experiences laid the foundation for my getting a job as after-school daycare counselor at a different YMCA in college. The lessons and experience gained in these volunteering gigs have led to a range of opportunities throughout my life, from working in residential programs to running a youth leadership program and book club for kids.

Audiobooks and Volunteering

"In hindsight, I can see the pattern happen again and again. I volunteer to do something, and it opens up a range of new opportunities. Audiobooks are a great example. I'm a bit of an audiobook evangelist. I've listened to thousands of them in my life and thoroughly enjoy a well-narrated story. So after graduating college, I was just as much an audiobook nut and saw it as an unexplored field for many. I wanted to get involved. So I looked about and found a site dedicated to audiobooks: Audiobook Café. In a desire to get involved, I emailed the site's executive director and said, 'Hey, I'll do whatever — can I volunteer for you?' They took me on as traffic coordinator. Basically, I had to get traffic directed to the site. Eventually, they let me write about audiobooks and review them for the site (and for that, they did pay me).

"Though the site's finances began to fall through, they helped me secure reviewer gigs at two magazines (which eventually expanded to three). Just a little more than a decade from when I started that venture, I have professionally written more than 800 audiobook reviews, conducted more than a dozen interviews with people in the industry, and written several articles on the subject. My interest went even further, and I eventually presented at the National

Popular Culture Association's annual conference in 2009 on the subject of audiobooks and Stephen King.

Comics and Volunteering

"I took a similar course with comics. As I got involved in reviewing audiobooks, I became curious about reviewing graphic novels, and so I contacted several sites to write graphic novel reviews, including CurledUp.com and Book-Loons.com. The general editors of these sites were kind and welcoming, took me in, and helped me get started. They provided support when needed and good editorial feedback where required. At the same time, I was in grad school, and a peer of mine made me aware that I could, in fact, study comics to some degree.

"As I finished grad school and continued to review graphic novels, I also started teaching at the college level. So with the background I had developed through education and volunteering, I offered up the idea of teaching a course on comics. This was successful enough to teach at four colleges and universities in the greater Boston area and regularly teach it at North Shore Community College.

"As I stepped into my new position at North Shore Community College, I wanted to make contacts and learn more about the different elements of instructional design. In particular, I've been interested in games and education. This led me eventually to learn about Media Grid: Immersive Education. I quickly joined the site and then also saw a conference in Boston in early June. Knowing that I couldn't get the funds for access to the conference, I contacted the organization to ask if I could volunteer and work at the conference in exchange for access. They agreed, and the doors opened.

"The experience opened up a great range of ideas and learning. It also connected me with a variety of great, exciting people. As the conference came to a close, the organizers asked if I would like to stay on for future conferences and help out. It was really kind and pretty cool as they made clear that they appreciated the effort and enthusiasm that I showed. So all this has me thinking, where will this lead me?

"Indeed, I'm not volunteering out of a true sense of charity. I'm volunteering because I'm interested and want more out of wherever it is that I'm volunteering. But I'm also not advancing my volunteering as a sign of sainthood (though the audiobook gods may be grateful for my singlehanded efforts to convert at least 20 people I know to using audiobooks regularly). Instead, I'm reflecting on the ways that volunteering has given me ample opportunity to explore further and profit (initially in an intellectual sense but later in a monetary and reputational sense) from the subject of my attention."

7

ALTRUISM IS NATURAL

THERE IS a common misconception that human beings are inherently greedy. We appear to be selfish, with strong desires to compete for wealth, prestige, and possessions. There are prevailing ideas that the majority of our actions are to help ourselves and our closest relatives. According to some evolutionary psychology theories, these modern human characteristics evolved during prehistoric times. We can imagine a harsh environment where humans competed for food and territory.

We typically portray this as a time of extreme rivalry, during which only specific characteristics that provided people with survival advantages were passed on to future generations. Those who could dominate and control were the ones who survived and gave those genes to their offspring. Since people's prosperity relied on their ability to obtain resources, there was bound to be competition between communities, leading to the emergence of bigotry and warfare.

This seems logical. However, the presumption upon which we base it is incorrect. Throughout the hunter-gatherer period, human populations were sparse while resources were abundant, so experts believe it was a predominantly peaceful existence. Most anthropologists now conclude that conflict is a relatively recent phenomenon in human culture, occurring around the time of the first farming settlements.[1] Once we settled down and started to store our food, we had more opportunities to take advantage and more goods to steal.

The oldest clear evidence of deadly group aggression is a mass grave discovered in Sudan's Jebel Sahaba district, near the Nile River. Experts believe it is about 13,000 years old. Twenty-four of the grave's 59 skeletons show signs of violence, such as hack marks and embedded stone points.

These violent characteristics have emerged so recently that an ecological or evolutionary explanation does not seem likely. The first humans arose in Africa around two million years ago. Homo sapiens, the first modern humans, evolved from their early hominid predecessors around 300,000 years ago. The first evidence of warlike behavior can be traced to just 13,000 years ago. Thus, the generous aspects of our personality are likely much more ingrained than the aggressive.

We can also look at modern hunter-gatherer societies that currently live in ways similar to those of prehistoric humans. They have strong political and sexual egalitarianism and typically share everything. They have strategies for maintaining equality by ensuring that class disparities do not exist.[2]

Men usually have no power over women in such communities. Women choose their own marriage partners, decide what kind of work they want to do, and work when they want. They also have custody rights over their children if their marriage fails. Many researchers concur that such decentralized cultures were common until a few thousand years ago when population increases prompted the emergence of agriculture.

Research reveals that biology has conditioned us to be kind and compassionate to one another, to a certain extent.[3] Many animals are also considered altruistic; it's not limited to humans. Even when offspring belong to members of other species, they often actively protect young they aren't related to.

Evolutionary biologist E.O. Wilson theorizes that our ancestors cooperated with one another because those groups that worked well together were most successful. These winning genes were then passed on to their descendants.[4] For instance, tribes that communicated well to devise the most efficient ways of obtaining food were those that survived.

We can also see evidence of altruistic behavior in infants and children. This is significant because it indicates behavior closely related to our biology rather than learned traits. Since infants are so fragile, they must learn to differentiate between those who can help and those who can harm them. Many academic groups have found that children as young as six to ten months of age selectively engage people who enact prosocial behaviors.[5]

Cooperative actions incite an early type of altruistic behavior in children as young as one to two years old, with the infants assisting strangers in obtaining an item out of their reach.[6] We have probably all encountered a child who tries to give us something they deem valuable. They even seem very pleased when we accept their offer. Children are capable of exchanging and expecting reciprocation by the age of five.[7]

Since the activity of helping others is likely in our genes, perhaps this is why some who seemingly have it all are still unsatisfied. Maybe we need to perform selfless actions to feel truly satisfied in our lives. Perhaps this is another reason we naturally feel gratified when working together to achieve a common goal that benefits everyone.

8

REAL-WORLD EXPERIENCES

KATHLEEN O'NEILL - SCHOOL librarian in Glasgow, Scotland[1]

Kathleen is a scholar-librarian who writes and researches. She also attends to the library and the information needs of others. These two sides of her career balance one another perfectly. When not at work, she is a volunteer tour guide at the Burrell Collection in Glasgow. She started guiding to help her overcome her fear of public speaking.

"The Burrell is one of my favorite museums, containing a fascinating range of medieval artifacts. I felt that it would be the best vehicle for my volunteering, as I already had an excellent medieval knowledge base. I was able to put my knowledge to good use and learn a great deal more about medieval art, as well as art up to the nineteenth century.

"This volunteer role, which I held for two years, brought some unexpected benefits: it improved my public speaking skills, and increased my confidence. I also got to know various curators, benefiting from their knowledge. I gained valuable experience and training in various aspects of art history, which helped me secure my first librarian role in the History of Art Department at Glasgow University.

"Since moving to London, I have continued to do volunteer work. In 2010, I spent almost every weekend between May and July acting as a steward at the Lambeth Palace Library. My main reason for applying for this role was to get myself known at the library, and to develop my career in rare book librarianship. I also wanted to continue developing my public speaking and presentation skills.

"It was a great opportunity, and I even had the chance to use my Old French and Latin skills to translate a page of *La*

Danse Macabre for an exhibition visitor. It was a valuable lesson in creating, maintaining, and administering a rare books exhibition.

"Like the majority of volunteer work, it is, of course, not entirely selfless and altruistic. I love to write; I am interested in the themes of these books and I want to make myself known to people working in the fields covered by these books.

"Unfortunately, I decided to leave these roles because I felt that it was impossible to do all that I wanted to do without the support, and better organization, of more senior committee members. Volunteering doesn't work if some people do not pull their weight and try to make things happen. In one respect, then, it was a frustrating few years. Still, in another, I gained a lot of confidence and experience in event planning, general administration, networking, and information sharing, all of which are transferable skills that I will use in my future career."

Volunteers in Bosnia-Herzegovina[2]

Through volunteerism, young people can learn new skills relevant to the workplace, as well as contribute their ideas and gain the practical expertise necessary to implement them. Moreover, volunteering provides direct access to working professionals and future contacts.

"My first professional full-time job happened because of my volunteer projects. I worked in a marketing team for one project, where I contacted a research company. Several months after the project, they contacted me themselves to ask me to work for them," says Nina Marković, former long-term volunteer, currently a brand manager in Sarajevo.

Marković goes on to explain how her volunteering experience enabled her to gain particular skills and knowledge to build a résumé with the potential to stand out from the crowd.

"Volunteering gave me firsthand practical knowledge; I signed my first contract, had my first job interview, planned projects, and was part of a team in addition to leading one. I did not have the chance to experience all of those things in my formal education. Our surroundings do not allow us to gain a lot of practical knowledge after finishing our studies, so volunteering is one of the easiest steps we can take and will make us more competitive in the labor market."

Asja Kratović, a long-term volunteer working for the National Democratic Institute in Bosnia, explains how volunteerism provides individuals with more opportunities for personal improvement, making them more capable and efficient.

"Volunteering was one of the main reasons I got numerous scholarships and fellowships for different summer schools, programs, trainings, master's studies, my first job, and all other jobs that followed. Volunteering provided me with a free educational and professional trip throughout Europe and the US. If I could go back and volunteer even more, then I would, because no book can teach you the things that you learn through hands-on experience."

Indeed, confident and capable applicants are more likely to be successful in securing jobs. Kratović further illustrates how, through volunteering, people develop communication and leadership skills, expand their social networks, and become more desirable applicants for future employment.

"My experience volunteering was something that gave me more credibility in every job to which I applied. Every employer wants to know that [their] employees are dedicated to working, and what better way to prove this than to work for free for a certain period. This will show them you are not only driven by money but also you believe in the mission and vision of this company. It indicates you will give the best of yourself to become a valuable member of their team."

Bosnia's cultural lack of volunteerism is due to insufficient support from institutions and unawareness of the positive effects of volunteering on the part of students. Academic institutions, in particular, are not providing enough information to potential volunteers.

"When I was a high school student, I knew very little about volunteering opportunities or academic and other exchange opportunities available for youth my age. I wasn't even aware of the various scholarships and funding opportunities that are open for youth to study at the world's most prestigious universities – something I now deeply regret not knowing," says Ilma Ibrišević, a long-term volunteer.

Volunteerism not only benefits those seeking hands-on experience but also the host institutions, as they can then employ volunteers who have gained the specific skills required by their institution through their voluntary experience. Post-Conflict Research Center (PCRC) is a Sarajevo-based NGO that alone had more than 30 young interns from around the world undertaking voluntary work with them throughout last year.

"Since 2011, when they founded the center, we have received more than 200 applications for internships, and we continue to receive new ones every day. These young people come from various countries within Europe and worldwide, but many are from Bosnia. Volunteers at our center are an amazing resource; they provide exceptional help in our work and the improvement of our projects," says Velma Šarić, executive director of PCRC.

Volunteerism can therefore enable individuals to display an ability to work successfully within a team, provide practical experience of situations requiring critical and analytical thinking, show proven flexibility and organizational skills, and foster innovation potential. These attributes may prove beneficial to applicants looking to secure paid employment in a job market where there is a high rate of unemployment while providing host institutions with passionate, dedicated individuals who can enhance their work in many ways. Further developing and encouraging a culture of volunteerism in Bosnia, therefore, appears to be a win-win situation.

Lule - Volunteer from Kosovo in Poland[3]

"We live every day with a vision for a better and more equal world that reaches everyone, but what actions do we take to achieve that? I believe that each daily action we take can make a difference, however small it is. All we have to do is find the most suitable practice. Volunteering is a perfect way to become aware of problems people struggle with and help solve them or make the problems smaller.

"The summer I volunteered, I received a message from a friend with an opportunity she had seen, an organization in Poland looking for a volunteer from Kosovo. I was immensely happy and excited. I started my application right away, and just days later, I got the confirmation email that my application had been accepted. It was a day I would hold dear.

"Before my departure, I needed to do many things to prepare, like finding a supporting organization. This took me a very long time, but all the wait was so worth it. I ended up having the best organization I could ever ask for, GAIA Kosovo. I still remember the day when I asked them to support me with my project. They agreed to support me right away. I can never thank them enough. Jeremy has helped me with everything since day one. I thank him kindly for all the support and help he has been giving.

"After all the time planning and organizing everything, in October I made my way to Poland. I was very excited, but also a little bit scared about what was waiting for me. It was my first time in a European country, and I had no idea how it would be. However, everything changed when I met the organization's director, mentors, and other volunteers. They welcomed me, and all my worries disappeared. I started living and working with ten people from different parts of Europe. I had the chance to learn a lot from them, share my experiences and listen to theirs. I learned a lot about our similarities and our differences as cultures, but also as countries.

"I worked in the office with different tasks related to office projects, supporting the organization with social media, workshops, and youth projects. I love what we are trying to do here and what impact we are trying to make on the youth of our local community. We're trying to promote youth integration and inclusion and emphasize the importance of their participation in the community for their good. I have seen what a crucial indicator youth can be and how much power we can have once we learn to use the tools we have and how to organize ourselves.

"Moreover, I enjoy my time with the other volunteers so much. Unfortunately, considering the situation we are in with the pandemic, we don't have many opportunities to travel around Poland. Still, we have been trying to make the best of what we already have. We live in a village near the mountains, and we have been exploring and hiking the mountains around us. We all learned that to have a great time, you can do so by just spending quality time with people.

"I have been here for almost five months now, and I can indeed say that I have grown and learned much more than I could in years. I had the chance to raise awareness of different social injustices and European projects and disseminate European values among young people. Other than that, I gained and improved many skills, such as teamwork, communication skills, the ability to adapt while working with different people, problem-solving, and improved interpersonal skills. It has been a fantastic experience so far. I learned and challenged myself in various ways.

"Being a volunteer has taught me that no small change is negligible. Maybe you won't see the results of your work right away, but you will eventually. It also taught me about solidarity, one of the core human values we all should have. It is the fundamental value to create a society of inclusion, social justice, and equality.

"To sum up, volunteering projects can and will change your life. What better way to learn than through experience and by helping a cause you value? For those volunteering in the future, I hope it will be as great an experience as mine was."

. . .

Volunteer Experiences of Moroccan, Turkish, and Surinamese Migrant Women[4]

Workfare volunteering is intended to contribute to the empowerment of migrant women. These interviews with the women show how empowerment is, in fact, an actual outcome of workfare volunteering. We will present empirical examples from the stories of Arhimou, Rowena, and Aliye. These are three examples of women representing three patterns of empowerment as an outcome of workfare volunteering.

However, the example of Aliye also shows how easily the situation can threaten empowerment. The example of Naomi shows when workfare volunteering results in feelings of disempowerment. The empirical models offer us five conditions that need to be present for volunteer work to empower migrant women.

The first condition under which volunteer work empowers migrant women is the possibility of putting trainer education or experience into practice. Arhimou, a Moroccan woman of 46 years old, has always been a housewife, but recently started working as a volunteer in a sewing group. She completed a course to become a seamstress before getting married back in Morocco, but she did not have the opportunity to use these skills after her marriage. Before the following excerpt, she proudly tells how she can help other women in the sewing class. She then goes on to explain how her confidence grew because of her volunteer work:

"Luckily, I can do all these things as a little handyman, haha. Yes, when I am there, I think sometimes, it is good that at least I took this sewing course when I was young. Then at least I have accomplished something for myself. Yes, it is a lot of fun. It is also mine; I always dreamed about really doing something like that, with sewing. Then I think yeah, some women go to work, everyone does something, but then I used to think, I am just sitting at home all by myself. I don't like that. If I look at my life right now, I'm really happy."

The opportunity to use her skills makes Arhimou feel appreciated and valued. This example shows how volunteering in itself can be a beneficial experience.

It is worth noting that to empower, volunteer work does not necessarily have to improve someone's employability. In Arhimou's case, volunteering does not contribute much to language attainment (the women in this group also speak predominantly Moroccan), learning new skills (she already knows how to sew), or finding paid employment. It does provide Arhimou with a source of meaning and purpose and the feeling of being valued.

A second condition under which volunteer work empowers migrant women is when it allows them to positively reframe their self-image. An example of a woman for whom volunteering is such an empowering experience is Rowena. Like Arhimou, Rowena can also use her former education, but more importantly, volunteering allows her to transform what she believes are her "weaknesses" into "strengths."

Rowena is 28 years old and of Surinamese descent (second generation). She is currently studying at a university but missed many years of study due to a severe car accident at the age of 22 that resulted in a lengthy coma, brain damage, and chronic physical pain. She tells how she experiences volunteering at a foundation for people with similar conditions.

"My condition always stood in the way of my studies, like water and fire. But here, when volunteering, they are both assets, you see? It is difficult to combine, but it also gives me energy. At the university, I sometimes feel like the difficult one, who needs more time, who needs special help. I always get it, but I don't want to need it. Before, I never needed it.

Well, here they know about my experience, and here it's an asset, that's why I got the job, they value it because I have firsthand experience with it [having brain damage]."

Volunteering allows her to use her major obstacle in life, her condition resulting from the car accident, as an asset. This particular volunteer job will enable her to transform herself from "the difficult one" into "the expert by experience." This has an empowering effect; it gives her strength and contributes to her confidence and self-esteem.

The third condition under which volunteer work empowers migrant women is when it allows them to work at their own pace and make mistakes. This resonates with previous research that found volunteer work offers welfare clients an empowering respite. Aliye, a Turkish second-generation migrant woman who suffered from depression after her husband died and she lost her job due to budget cuts, describes clearly how the absence of pressure enables her to build confidence and self-esteem.

"Well, I wasn't ready for a job because a paid job also comes with extra pressure. You have to achieve. So yeah, that's why I don't mind so much if I make a little mistake here. But when I just started here, I was very insecure. I was always like, oh no, am I doing everything right? But they are very relaxed here. They said yes, you are doing everything well. Don't worry, just do your thing. So yeah, that helped me."

Empowering Social Capital

A fourth condition under which volunteer work empowers is when it contributes to migrant women's bonding social capital. Most of the organizations where our respondents volunteer are based in specific neighborhoods, often the less well-off neighborhoods in the bigger cities. As such, the people our respondents meet often have similar educational backgrounds and financial situations. Latifa describes how the people who work at the community center where she volunteers help each other:

"Many people around here struggle. They have no job, depend on social welfare, or have financial issues. But that is also the good thing; we all understand that. If someone can't make it because there is no money left to pay for a bus ticket to the community center, then someone else picks her up, like that. We've all been there, tough times, so it is good we can support each other here."

The migrant women highly value having bonding social capital. Understanding each other, being able to be yourself, and providing support in case of difficulties benefit several women. Volunteering may provide bonding social capital, but not the bridging social capital associated with finding employment. Without an increasing chance to return to the labor market, volunteering eventually disempowers these women.

Disempowering Expectations

The previous examples show how and under which conditions volunteering leads to empowerment. However, about a third of the women have the opposite experience. When the above-mentioned conditions — the possibilities of using skills, reframing self-image, absence of pressure, or bonding social capital — are no longer present, volunteering may result in disempowerment. This happens mostly when volunteering does not contribute to the prospect of having a paid job.

In several cases, we noticed how increasing expectations contradicted empowerment, such as finding paid employment. To Aliye, for instance, volunteer work and paid work are not the same thing. Quite the opposite: She feels volunteer work offers her an escape from the pressure of doing paid work.

"But now welfare officials say, oh you are volunteering, then you can also have a paid job. But this is my own thing. It is bizarre if you punish people who are actively trying to get back into that work rhythm, who want to do something valuable. Yeah, also to become a bit more secure of themselves."

The pressure welfare officials put on Aliye to find paid employment contradicts the empowering effect of the absence of pressure at her volunteer job. The focus on paid work seems to overshadow her accomplishment of volunteering to deal with losing her spouse and suffering from depression. Instead of encouragement, she feels like they punish her for her efforts. The pressure by Aliye's caseworker disempowers her.

A second reason why volunteer work disempowers migrant women is that not being paid may eventually contribute to feeling used. So, in the long run, there is a fifth condition that needs to be present for volunteer work to empower migrant women: eventually, it needs to pay off.

Naomi, a first-generation Surinamese migrant, has recently lost her job and picked up volunteering with the vague promise of paid employment at the organization where she volunteers. At first, helping people empowered her, but eventually, the feeling of being used got the upper hand:

"Yeah, I don't mind [working unpaid] for a few months, but if they think you are so great and you have been working there for a while and then they say, 'Oh, sorry, we cannot pay you,' but they do want you to do all kinds of things and work hard, then I feel a bit like, that they are using you, yeah, hahaha! I mean, it is great to help people, but you can only help others if you can sustain yourself."

Especially the idea of being taken advantage of seems to disempower Naomi. She explains why it matters who is profiting from her kindness:

"You know, I don't mind volunteering for people who have nothing, the poor, the elderly, the disabled, but for organizations who have tons of money but just feel like not paying you, that I don't like. Then I don't feel valued, you know. You have to do volunteer work from the heart. And not something like, okay, we think you do a great job, but we are not going to pay you."

For Naomi, the experience of volunteering for an organization with the means to pay her is disempowering. She feels valued when helping others, but only under the condition of being in a position of financial security.

Rosa Blumenfeld - Canadian woman who volunteered at a cooperative village in Israel[5]

"During the past two and a half months, I have been a volunteer here at Neve Shalom/Wahat al-Salam (NSWAS). I was the first volunteer working with the public relations office as the assistant to the current director. I would be working with the group's coordinator cleaning a lot and performing odd jobs. I was both excited at this new opportunity but also quite nervous as well. All kinds of questions were running through my head: Will I be good enough to stay here for an extended period? Will people like me? What exactly will my work be? How are the other volunteers, etc?

"Although cleaning toilets is a powerful motivation to go to a new place, I came to NSWAS because I identified with its ideology. I knew that the work would be challenging, but I was looking forward to doing something new. It turned out that there were actually quite a few that I needed to clean here, a process which I have performed several times and which I will no doubt continue doing until the end of my stay here.

"With that, I entered into a new routine: Sundays and Tuesdays were PR days, and Mondays, Wednesdays, and Thursdays were cleaning days. Two days meant coming to work in nice clothes to be presentable around the office, and the other three consisted of wearing sweatpants and baggy t-shirts.

"Working at the PR office consisted of translating, writing emails and thank-you letters, and researching information online that could potentially benefit NSWAS. Working with the groups coordinator consisted of cleaning the entire office building, preparing the auditorium for incoming groups (including the adjoining bathrooms), and doing other projects in and around the building.

It took me a little while to get used to the rhythm of the work. I knew coming in that it would be hard and physical work, so I struggled with it initially, and slowly, as I got more used to it, my pace quickened, and I started to feel more at ease at work.

"After hours, I spent time with the other volunteers and people around my age living in the village. They invited me for coffee, dinner, and just to chat. Within the first few weeks, a family adopted me in the village whose daughter is a very good friend. I went to the Purim party at Kibbutz Nachshon with the younger people of the village and another volunteer. Once I got home from work, I had time to sit and read, visit with people and get acquainted, which I felt I didn't have time for as a full-time student.

"Before I knew it, I had already been here for a month, then two, and now I am fast approaching the third month of my stay here.

Although both jobs I have been doing differ quite a bit, I have learned a lot about the village, and also myself as a person, from each of them. I realized that although they founded this village on ideals, it is not perfect. It is a community with its problems, disagreements, and politics, just like any other community.

Although two very different peoples live here together, the lines that sometimes divide the community around specific issues aren't based on religion or nationality but rather on the people themselves and their opinions.

"One of the most exciting things for me is talking to actual Palestinians and listening to what they have to say. This is a process that I never had the opportunity to do before as a Canadian Jew even though I lived in Israel for a couple of years as a child. I have also learned about the typically negative attitude the Israeli government has about this place. The consequences are that they privately fund almost everything that they accomplish here. The Israeli government does provide some funding but not nearly enough for the village to sustain itself.

"It was difficult for me to realize that the government of a state that I believe in so much could have such a negative attitude toward a place like Neve Shalom/Wahat al-Salam. I also learned about the different things that happen in this village that coincide with their goal of peaceful coexistence, such as the School for Peace, the workings of the elementary and junior high schools, and the Doumia/Skina. I have also learned about the history of this place and current issues within the village.

"Now that almost three months have gone by, and as I reflect upon my time spent here, I realize that even though this place has its imperfections it is essential to keep in mind precisely what an accomplishment it is, an accomplishment that came out of nothing.

As I look around at the situation in Israel and the Middle East, living here at Neve Shalom/Wahat al-Salam gives me hope that the futures of both the Palestinians and Jews living here in Israel can be brighter."

Older Adults' Volunteer Experiences[6]

As the numbers of older adults in developed countries grow, it becomes increasingly necessary to look at aging differently than we've done in the past. In 2019, about 16.5 percent of the US population was 65 or older, which will likely rise to 22 percent by 2050. This represents a substantial increase from 1950 when just 8 percent of the population was 65 or older.[7]

Policy focus worldwide is shifting from attention on dependency, frailty, and poor health, commonly thought of as related to aging, toward awareness about healthy, productive aging and quality of life.[8]

One indication of productive aging is volunteering. In 2015, 24 percent of older adults volunteered. This equates to 11.0 million volunteers, 1.9 billion hours, and 45.4 billion dollars of service contributed.[9] While these numbers are encouraging, this also means that 76 percent of older American adults didn't volunteer.

While there are many studies on the benefits of volunteering for older adults, we don't yet know how these older adults *become* volunteers. Understanding how older adults volunteer is meaningful if service agencies hope to have more senior volunteers.

The purpose of this study is to explain the method by which older adults become volunteers. "Become" as utilized in this study may describe how these older adults incorporate volunteering into who they are and not just what they are doing. Most senior volunteers did not apply the term "volunteer" to themselves; instead, they saw themselves as people who "help out."

It was apparent that helping out described common patterns of interaction among the participants. They also talked about years of helping out that began back in childhood.

They named many motivations for volunteering. One was a desire to transmit values of caring that participants had learned earlier in their lives and to pass on blessings they had received.

Many participants related early childhood memories of working together with their parents to help out needy neighbors or do church work. These older adults felt a solid connection to others through their churches and organizational involvements.

Belonging to a group that was committed to volunteering was a strong motivator for the participants to volunteer. "Commitment" described the participants' sense of personal responsibility to help others. For many, this sense of commitment had roots in their Christian beliefs.

Almost all participants told of a sense of duty to help others. Jeannie, an 80-year-old woman with a lifelong connection to the Catholic church, described her commitment to helping out:

"I helped my mother. My mother was the church cleaner in the Catholic church, so I think that's where I got my volunteering from."

Tom, 68, who grew up in a rural community, shared how his previous experience influenced his helping out:

"Most of the folks working with our bunch grew up in the era when you helped your neighbor, too."

Joe, 72, a 40-year member of a fraternal organization that encourages its members to volunteer, described how belonging to the organization influenced his decisions in helping out:

"They are like a bunch of brothers, you know... and it's just a good feeling to be part of a (civic) group.

"I kinda feel a personal responsibility ... I just feel led. That's what I need to do. I am my brother's keeper."

Mike, 68, a retired life insurance salesman, echoed this sense of connection to others and a commitment arising from spiritual beliefs.

"I love people, and I've never had the heart to say no, I guess, so I volunteer when I can. God's got a whole lot for me to do, and I feel like this is a part of it."

Antecedent

Before the process of helping out could begin, an antecedent event had to occur. The antecedent to the entire process recognized a need. This recognition of a condition could come in two ways: Either an organization or individual asked for help, or the older adults saw a need to meet individually or with others.

Some participants were reluctant to help unless personally requested to do so, while others actively sought opportunities to help others. Ron, 70, a retired welder, described how he recognized opportunities for helping out:

"Well, I've learned that I have to fill in where it needs to be filled in ... I'm willing to do it."

Ron's wife, Julie, 69, described how she was willing to help out and anticipated someone asking her to help out every day:

"I've found out — what's the use of planning out your day? As soon as the first telephone rings, you know, the whole day is gone because somebody needs me. I don't think you would think twice about doing something for your neighbor, your friend, whoever is in need. I've never been any other way."

Jerry, 82, who was less outgoing, did not actively seek opportunities to help out. He described his reluctance to help out unless someone asked him to do so:

"If somebody says, 'I need your help,' I'll help them. If they don't ask, why, I don't butt in. That's it!"

Action/Interaction Strategy

Once a need is recognized, participants begin a deliberative process of choosing to help. Mary, 65, assisted several neighbors much older than her by running errands and taking them to appointments. She described her feelings about choosing to help out: "But these are genuine people that need help. They know they can depend on me."

Tom described his past personal experience of being poor and needing help himself at one time and how it influenced his decisions to help out:

"I love to help people that, you know, I feel like they appreciate it and they need it. Because I came from being very poor, so now if I see somebody that I know needs help, who's got several children, and they've become divorced or widowed — I know they need help, you know."

Consequences

Participants described the result of helping out as being blessed. The words "blessed" or "blessings" were used frequently by participants when they explained the benefits of volunteering. Participants related these as general blessings or as spiritual, social, emotional, or physical benefits gained from helping out.

More importantly, these blessings reinforced their volunteering and strengthened the contextual categories of continuity, connection, and commitment, increasing the likelihood that the older volunteer would volunteer again.

Blessings also increased the likelihood that these older volunteers would actively seek future opportunities to volunteer and choose to help if asked. In fact, the more they helped out, the more they wanted to help out. Julie related blessings she received from volunteering:

"You do something that they ask you to do and you are accomplishing something, and you feel good about yourself."

Sam stated that he looked every day for an opportunity to help others. He related:

"It just feels good to share the blessings that you had in your life. I would recommend this to anybody who wanted a blessing out of life. I feel blessed, and it is good to share some of your blessings with somebody else."

Carl, a very active 82-year-old, discussed blessings in terms of the physical and mental benefits of volunteering.

"Well, it will probably make you get more exercise than you would ordinarily. So that helps you, physical exercise and mind and everything else."

· · ·

Darren - Volunteer at Mind, a mental health charity in the United Kingdom[10]

"I've been suffering from mental health problems since I was 17 years old. I found it impossible to hold down a job, a relationship, or enjoy any kind of social life. Then I found out about the Mind for Mental Health team. Once referred, I started going to a local gardening project. Staff and members alike instantly made me feel welcome. After being a member for about a year, I began to drive a couple of days a week, taking members to horse riding outings and outreach projects.

"My confidence started to grow, and I began to help out in the center a couple of days a week. I was helping members with internet research, setting up smartphones and email accounts, sometimes just a chat and a coffee. It gives me a great sense of satisfaction to give my time to an organization that has helped me so much. I can manage my mental health a bit better than I could a few years ago, and this is thanks primarily to Mind and the people with whom they've put me in touch.

"If I'm having a bad day or find something is too much, there's always someone there. The flexibility of volunteering allows me to attend my appointments and manage my mental health when needed. I've also done some campaigning through Mind to break mental health stigma and give people a voice. It helps other people to know that they're not alone and there are other people like us.

"I can recommend volunteering to anyone. You can make a difference in someone else's life and make their day that little bit easier, and it's excellent for you."

Thank you for reading my book! I hope it helps you. It would mean a great deal to me if you take a moment and write a review on Amazon. To stay up to date on my future book releases sign up for my email list:

janelcsterbentz.com/subscribe/

9

RESOURCES

AARP CREATE the Good

createthegood.aarp.org

Create the Good connects you with volunteer opportunities to share your life experiences, skills, and passions in your community.

All for Good

allforgood.org

Search for events, projects, and organizations near you from volunteer sites all around the web. Register your organization and manage volunteer signups. Start projects on your own, for your community.

. . .

AmeriCorps

americorps.gov

AmeriCorps members and AmeriCorps Seniors volunteers directly serve nonprofit organizations to tackle our nation's most pressing challenges.

Catchafire

catchafire.org

Catchafire strengthens the social good sector by matching professionals who want to donate their time with nonprofits who need their skills.

Do Something

dosomething.org

As the largest not-for-profit exclusively for young people and social change, DoSomething's millions of members represent every US area code and 131 countries. DoSomething members join our volunteer, social change, and civic action campaigns to make a real-world impact on relevant causes using our digital platform.

Encore.org

encore.org

Encore.org is a nonprofit dedicated to bridging divides, connecting across generations, and creating a better future together. We work to change the culture by elevating new ideas and diverse voices on the power of connection and collaboration across generational divides.

Feeding America

feedingamerica.org/take-action/volunteer

For more than 40 years, Feeding America has responded to the needs of individuals struggling with food insecurity in this country. In times of uncertainty, we have not wavered from our mission to end the fight against hunger.

GiveGab

givegab.com

The number one digital solution for connecting people with the causes they care about through Giving Days and year-round fundraising.

GivePulse

givepulse.com

Our mission is to enable everyone in the world to participate and engage in lifting their community to new heights. We do so by providing a platform to list, find, and organize opportunities, and measure the impact of service-learning, community engagement, philanthropy, and volunteerism in the community.

GozAround

gozaround.com

GozAround is a network for people, businesses, and nonprofits looking to make a difference in their unique way. Whether that's through a virtual volunteer role, helping someone down the street, offsetting your carbon footprint, or simply making a donation, we believe giving back should be easy and personalized.

Golden Volunteer

goldenvolunteer.com

Volunteer and organize the future you envision with easy, powerful, and award-winning volunteer management software.

Globe Aware

globeaware.org

Globe Aware is a nonprofit that develops short-term volunteer programs in international environments that encourage people to immerse themselves in a unique way of giving back.

Habitat for Humanity

habitat.org/volunteer

A global nonprofit housing organization working in local communities across all 50 states in the US and approximately 70 countries. Habitat's vision is of a world where everyone has a decent place to live. Habitat works toward our vision by building strength, stability, and self-reliance in partnership with families in need of decent and affordable housing. Habitat homeowners help build their own homes alongside volunteers and pay an affordable mortgage.

International Volunteer HQ

volunteerhq.org

At International Volunteer HQ, we bring people from more than 150 countries to create positive transformation through life-enriching travel experiences. This transformation takes place not just within the communities we support but also within volunteers themselves.

· · ·

Jumpstart

jstart.org/about

Jumpstart is a national early education organization working toward the day every child in America enters kindergarten prepared to succeed. We provide language, literacy, and social-emotional programming for preschool children from under-resourced communities and promote quality early learning for all children. Since 1993, we've trained more than 50,000 college students and community volunteers to transform the lives of more than 123,000 preschool children nationwide.

JustServe

justserve.org

Volunteers can search for places to serve in the community, providing opportunities to help those in need and enhance the quality of life in the community.

Kids That Do Good

kidsthatdogood.com

An online database founded by kids, it lists local, regional, and national volunteer opportunities appropriate for children.

· · ·

Points of Light

pointsoflight.org

An international nonpartisan nonprofit organization based
in the US, it connects volunteers to social issues that interest
them.

Red Cross

redcross.org/volunteer/become-a-volunteer.html

Volunteers perform 90% of their humanitarian work. Volunteer opportunities include supporting blood donations and
delivering much-needed services to your community. There
is also a wide variety of remote opportunities available.

Taproot Foundation

taprootfoundation.org

Taproot Foundation, a national nonprofit, connects
nonprofits and social change organizations with passionate
business professionals who share their expertise pro bono.
Taproot is creating a world where organizations dedicated to
social change have full access — through pro bono service
— to the marketing, strategy, HR, and IT resources they need
to be most effective.

. . .

United Way

unitedway.org/get-involved/volunteer

United Way envisions a world where every individual has an opportunity to succeed, and entire communities thrive as a result. We're getting a little closer every day, with help from millions of people around the world.

VolunteerMatch

volunteermatch.org

Engages volunteers to work on local causes.

NOTES

1. Introduction

1. Downs S. "How Volunteering Changed My Life." *Make Life Good*, 22 Dec. 2018, Copyright 2018, Use of article granted 12 May 2021, makelifegood. org/how-volunteering-changed-my-life. materialinnovation.org/.

2. How Does Helping Others Help Me?

1. Anderson ND, Damianakis T, Kröger E, Wagner LM, Dawson DR, Binns S, Bernstein S, Caspi E, Cook SL. "The Benefits Associated With Volunteering Among Seniors: A Critical Review and Recommendations for Future Research." *Psychological Bulletin*, U.S. National Library of Medicine, 25 Aug. 2014, pubmed.ncbi.nlm.nih.gov/25150681/.
2. Harris A, Thoresen C. "Volunteering Is Associated With Delayed Mortality in Older People: Analysis of the Longitudinal Study of Aging." *SAGE Journals*, 1 Dec. 2005, journals.sagepub.com/doi/abs/10.1177/1359105305057310/.
3. Leigh-Hunt N, et al. "An Overview of Systematic Reviews on the Public Health Consequences of Social Isolation and Loneliness." *Public Health*, 12 Sept. 2017, sciencedirect.com/science/article/abs/pii/S0033350617302731?via%3Dihub/.
4. "Loneliness Is at Epidemic Levels in America." Cigna, 2020, cigna.com/about-us/newsroom/studies-and-reports/combatting-loneliness/.
5. "UnitedHealthcare Study Finds Americans Who Volunteer Feel Healthier and Happier." UnitedHealth Group, 24 Feb. 2020, unitedhealthgroup.com/newsroom/2017/0914studydoinggoodisgoodforyou.html/.
6. Miller KD, Schleien SJ, Rider C, Hall C, Roche M, Worsley J. "Inclusive volunteering: Benefits to participants and community." Jan. 2002. *American Psychological Association*, psycnet.apa.org/record/2002-11232-003/.
7. UnitedHealth Group. "UnitedHealthcare Study Finds Americans Who Volunteer Feel Healthier and Happier." 24 Feb. 2020, unitedhealth-

group.com/viewer.html?file=/content/dam/UHG/PDF/2017/2017_Study-Doing-Good-is-Good-for-You.pdf.

8. Trew JL, Alden LE. "Kindness reduces avoidance goals in socially anxious individuals." *Motivation and Emotion.* 5 Jun. 2015, psycnet.apa.org/record/2015-25707-001/.

9. Poulin MJ, Holman AE. "Helping Hands, Healthy Body? Oxytocin Receptor Gene and Prosocial Behavior Interact to Buffer the Association Between Stress and Physical Health." *Hormones and Behavior*, Academic Press, 24 Jan. 2013, sciencedirect.com/science/article/abs/pii/S0018506X13000202/.

10. Universität Bonn. "Oxytocin Helps to Better Overcome Fear." *ScienceDaily*, ScienceDaily, 13 Nov. 2014, sciencedaily.com/releases/2014/11/141113110014.htm/.

11. Anderson ND, Damianakis T, Kröger E, Wagner LM, Dawson DR, Binns MA, Bernstein S, Caspi E, Cook SL, "The Benefits Associated With Volunteering Among Seniors: a Critical Review and Recommendations for Future Research." *Psychological Bulletin*, U.S. National Library of Medicine, 25 Aug. 2014, pubmed.ncbi.nlm.nih.gov/25150681/.

12. Salt E, Crofford LJ, Segerstrom S. "The Mediating and Moderating Effect of Volunteering on Pain and Depression, Life Purpose, Well-Being, and Physical Activity." *Pain Management Nursing: Official Journal of the American Society of Pain Management Nurses*, U.S. National Library of Medicine, 7 Jun. 2017, pubmed.ncbi.nlm.nih.gov/28601476/.

13. Wang Y, et al. "Altruistic Behaviors Relieve Physical Pain." *PNAS*, National Academy of Sciences, 14 Jan. 2020, pnas.org/content/117/2/950/.

14. Rea S. "Volunteering Reduces Risk of Hypertension in Older Adults" Carnegie Mellon University, *Science Daily*, 13 Jun. 2013, sciencedaily.com/releases/2013/06/130613092344.htm/.

15. Alvord M, et al. "Manage Stress: Strengthen Your Support Network." *American Psychological Association*, 8 Oct. 2019, apa.org/topics/stress/manage-social-support/.

16. Noonan SJ. "Volunteer When Depressed? The Life You Save May Be Your Own." *Psychology Today*, Sussex Publishers, Copyright - June 18, 2016, Use of article granted 11 May 2021, psychologytoday.com/us/blog/view-the-mist/201606/volunteer-when-depressed-the-life-you-save-may-be-your-own/, susannoonanmd.com/.

3. How Do I Start?

1. "What It's Like to Be: a Teen Volunteer at a Hospital." YouTube, 11 Aug. 2019, Creative Commons: creativecommons.org/licenses/by/3.0/, edited for clarity, youtu.be/kiDhucMksLE/.

4. Volunteering

1. Mogilner C. "You'll Feel Less Rushed If You Give Time Away." *Harvard Business Review*, 27 Sept. 2017, hbr.org/2012/09/youll-feel-less-rushed-if-you-give-time-away/.

2. UnitedHealth Group. "UnitedHealthcare Study Finds Americans Who Volunteer Feel Healthier and Happier." 24 Feb. 2020, unitedhealth-group.com/newsroom/2017/0914studydoinggoodisgoodforyou.html/.

3. "Volunteering in U.S. Hits Record High; Worth $167 Billion." Corporation for National and Community Service, 13 Nov. unitedhealthgroup.-com/viewer.html?file=/content/dam/UIIG/PDF/2017/2017_Study-Doing-Good-is-Good-for-You.pdf/

4. Moll J, et al. "Human Fronto-Mesolimbic Networks Guide Decisions about Charitable Donation." *Proceedings of the National Academy of Sciences,* pnas.org/content/103/42/15623/

5. "How Volunteering Changed My Life." YouTube, 11 Mar. 2021, Copyright 2021: Use of content granted 13 May 2021, youtu.be/h6aAV__kMeo/.

5. Tips for Volunteering

1. Dunn E, Norton M. *Happy Money: The Science of Smarter Spending.* Simon & Schuster Paperbacks, 2014.

2. Eisner D, et al. "The New Volunteer Workforce." Winter 2009, *Stanford Social Innovation Review: Informing and Inspiring Leaders of Social Change,* ssir.org/articles/entry/the_new_volunteer_workforce/.

3. Bruno F. "The Community: Volunteer for the Blind." YouTube, 27 July 2020, Creative Commons: creativecommons.org/licenses/by/3.0/, edited for clarity, youtu.be/1b-r3adSJ5I/.

6. Turn Your Passion Into Money

1. Corporation for National and Community Service, nationalservice.gov/vcla/research/.
2. "Business Formation Statistics." Census.gov, 10 Jun. 2021, census.gov/econ/bfs/pdf/bfs_current.pdf/.
3. "State of Independence." MBO Partners, 1 Apr. 2021, mbopartners.com/state-of-independence/.
4. Hofschneider A. "How Altruism Could Help Get You Hired, The *Wall Street Journal*, 7 Aug. 2013, wsj.com/articles/BL-ATWORKB-1139/.
5. "Volunteering in the United States," U.S. Bureau of Labor Statistics, 25 Feb. 2016, bls.gov/news.release/volun.htm/.
6. Eaton L. "Sure, I'll Do That: Where Volunteering Has Led Me," Blogger, 13 Aug. 2020, Creative Commons: creativecommons.org/licenses/by/3.0/, edited for clarity, www.byanyothernerd.com/2012/07/sure-i-do-that-where-volunteering-has.html.

7. Altruism Is Natural

1. Horgan J. "New Study of Prehistoric Skeletons Undermines Claim That War Has Deep Evolutionary Roots." Scientific American Blog Network, *Scientific American,* 24 July 2013, blogs.scientificamerican.com/cross-check/new-study-of-prehistoric-skeletons-undermines-claim-that-war-has-deep-evolutionary-roots/.
2. Knauft B, et al. "Violence and Sociality in Human Evolution." *Current Anthropology,* Aug–Oct. 1991, journals.uchicago.edu/doi/abs/10.1086/203975?journalCode=ca&/.
3. Filkowski MM, et al. "Altruistic Behavior: Mapping Responses in the Brain." *Neuroscience and Neuroeconomics*, U.S. National Library of Medicine, 2016, ncbi.nlm.nih.gov/pmc/articles/PMC5456281/.
4. Wilson EO, et al. "The evolution of eusociality." *Nature,* Vol. 466, No. 7310, 26 Aug. 2010, nature.com/articles/nature09205/.
5. Van de Vondervoort JW, Hamlin JK. "The Early Emergence of Sociomoral Evaluation: Infants Prefer Prosocial Others." *Current opinion in psychology.* U.S. National Library of Medicine, 12 Aug. 2017, pubmed.ncbi.nlm.nih.gov/28858770/.
6. Barragan RC, Carol SD. "Rethinking natural altruism: Simple reciprocal interactions trigger children's benevolence" *PNAS*, National Academy of Sciences, 2 Dec. 2014, pnas.org/content/111/48/17071/.

7. Sebastián-Enesco C, Warneken F. "The Shadow of the Future: 5-Year-Olds, but Not 3-Year-Olds, Adjust Their Sharing in Anticipation of Reciprocation." *Journal of Experimental Child Psychology*, U.S. National Library of Medicine, 19 Sept. 2014, pubmed.ncbi.nlm.nih.gov/25240748/ .

8. Real-World Experiences

1. O'Neill K. "Volunteering for Volunteering's Sake, & Volunteering for Your Career." The Victorian Librarian, 7 Jan. 2015, Creative Commons: creativecommons.org/licenses/by/3.0, edited for clarity, victorianlibrarian.wordpress.com/2012/12/30/volunteering-for-volunteerings-sake-and-volunteering-for-your-career-cpd23-thing-22-volunteering-to-gain-experience/.

2. Krkic L, et al. "The Benefits of Volunteerism for the Youth of Bosnia-Herzegovina." *Balkan Diskurs*, 23 Jan. 2021, Creative Commons: creativecommons.org/licenses/by/3.0, edited for clarity, balkandiskurs.com/en/2015/03/20/the-benefits-of-volunteerism-for-the-youth-of-bosnia-herzegovina/.

3. Lule. "The Story of Lule – ESC Volunteer in Poland." GAIA Kosovo, Mar. 2021, Creative Commons: creativecommons.org/licenses/by/4.0/, edited for clarity, gaiakosovo.org/2021/03/29/the-story-of-lule-esc-volunteer-in-poland/.

4. Slootjes J, Kampen T. "Is My Volunteer Job Not Real Work? The Experiences of Migrant Women with Finding Employment Through Volunteer Work." *Voluntas* 28, Creative Commons: creativecommons.org/licenses/by/4.0/, edited for clarity, link.springer.com/article/10.1007/s11266-017-9885-6/

5. Blumenfeld R. "Experience of a Volunteer in NSWAS." Wahat Al-Salam - Neve Shalom, 17 Jan. 2020, Creative Commons: creativecommons.org/licenses/by/3.0/, edited for clarity, wasns.org/experience-of-a-volunteer-in-nswas/.

6. Witucki JB, et al. "Becoming an Older Volunteer: A Grounded Theory Study." *Nursing Research and Practice*, Hindawi, 27 Dec. 2010, Creative Commons: creativecommons.org/licenses/by/3.0/, edited for clarity, hindawi.com/journals/nrp/2011/361250/.

7. "U.S. - Seniors as a Percentage of the Population 2050." *Statista*, 20 Jan. 2021, statista.com/statistics/457822/share-of-old-age-population-in-the-total-us-population/.

8. Angus J, Reeve P. "Ageism: a threat to aging well in the 21st century." *Journal of Applied Gerontology,* 1 Apr. 2006, journals.sagepub.com/doi/10.1177/0733464805285745/.

9. "Older Adults (Age 65+)." Corporation for National and Community Service, nationalservice.gov/vcla/demographic/older-adults-age-65/.

10. "How Volunteering Helped My Mental Health: Darren's Mental Health Story for #Volunteersweek: Mind." YouTube, 2 June 2015, Copyright 2015: Use of content granted 13 May 2021, youtu.be/AgI-c2je-6o, mind.org.uk/.

ABOUT THE AUTHOR

Janel Clare Sterbentz has a master's degree in urban studies and a bachelor's in sociology. She's volunteered for many organizations throughout her life and has even turned two of her passions into successful businesses. As founder of GreenEdge Studios, Janel has produced, filmed, and edited countless videos showcasing people and organizations working to improve their communities and the world. In San Francisco, she spearheaded projects to create greenlight corridors so cyclists could bike without encountering red lights. She founded and served as executive director of the bicycle advocacy group Bike San Antonio, which brought together a diverse coalition of people to make cycling in the city safer and more enjoyable. It led to millions of dollars being devoted to protected bike lanes.

Whether you are content with your life, yet feel like something is missing, or you are extremely depressed, the first step to satisfaction is to decide to make a change. Then learn about ways to improve your life. Through evidence based research, this book presents ways to establish better relationships with our friends, romantic partners, our bodies and our minds. Even if you are happy now, it's wise to collect tools to keep in your back pocket if life takes an unexpected turn. This will give you more control over aspects of your life that don't serve you. The healthier the individual, the stronger the society, which benefits everyone.